B$LLIONAIRE
BAD BOY

A MASTER'S COURSE
IN ACHIEVING THE
IMPOSSIBLE

Ray Bolden

ISBN-978-0-578-66238-1   (Bold Ambition Worldwide, LLC)

Dedication

This is dedicated to anyone and everyone who is struggling to see beyond what's right in front of them. The answers are inside of you. Wealth awaits all those who discover their true identity.

Author's Note

It's not about possessing things, money or titles. It's about developing the mindset and attitude to give yourself the ultimate power.

Table of Contents

Preface

When most people see rich people, they assume that they have some magical quality. There's an inherent feeling that excellence looks a certain way, it acts a certain way and that it came from a particular place. The problem is that most people just don't understand how the person got so rich. If you knew what that person did behind the scenes to get where they are, you'd think, "I can do that too!" It's not magic. Why? Because you are different, unique and unlike everyone else. Your personal story is your brand and I'm going to teach you how to monetize it. The lifestyle you want is not out of reach, you just don't know the moves yet. I'm sharing everything that anyone can apply to gain wealth and get what they want out of life in this course, so you can create your own magic. Right here within these pages is a wonderful opportunity for you to learn the truth about yourself...the truth of who you can be, what you can do and what you can have in your life. Through this powerful course, you can discover the power that is within you and learn how to use that power to be what you want to be, do what you want to do and have what you want to have. This study guide is a natural extension of the *BAD BOYS FINI$H RICH* series of books. In fact, its a compilation of the mind-set, attitude and action steps of all six books...the best of. Its execution follows the exact patterns that counter conventional business wisdom and these patterns directly correlate to wealth, freedom and a lot of winning. The power of money is within you and *B$LLIONAIRE BAD BOY* introduces you to it's presence. By studying the teachings contained in this course you can begin a new, more creative, more abundant life, right here and right now. The questions within this study guide have eternal applicability...they should not be limited. I realized that I was a Capitalist the moment I started to answer these questions, saw my opportunity, went for it and never looked back. I turned off the TV and stopped listening to the radio and thought about my life. I knew that if I continued to surrender, I would be allowing others to dictate my financial future forever. My only choice was to try to find the power that was in me and use it to empower myself economically...which is exactly what I did. You have to make choices based on the life you want to live now. It's not only a social and personal act but an economic act. Forget the rules and what anybody else is telling you that you should be doing with your life because your answers will surprise the hell out of you. Once you learn who you really are, you'll realize that building wealth is so easy, it's unbelievable. This course can help you to learn how to achieve the kind of life that you want to have, but you must study and practice these principles regularly. If you feel that you thoroughly absorb the ideas, feel free to progress at your own rate, but don't forget to go back again and again to previous lessons. This study guide is not designed to be read only once and then put away. Financial literacy and economic empowerment involve continual study and practice, so set aside a special time each day for reading and answering the questions. I suggest reading before you go to sleep at night to give your subconscious mind the opportunity to absorb these positive ideas while you sleep. Study and work the appendix questions and continually review them to determine if your answers align with your goals and aspirations. Say them out loud to yourself. This helps to reinforce these positive ideas in your subconscious mind and causes you to clearly define yourself in positive terms.

As you answer the questions, visualize yourself with the things you desire and the feeling of already having them. Continue to study and practice your answers every day. This will develop your financial literacy, empower you economically, reinforce the benefits of self-reliance and allow you to put newly discovered ideas into practice. Whether you form a study group or study on an individual basis, let the positive thoughts and ideas in this course become a part of you and practice them with faith. No more taking the easy way out! It's time to grow the fuck up. There is no more time to waste. Hours and days evaporate. These teachings can help you transform your way of thinking, and transform your way of life. Take full advantage of this opportunity to live a new, more abundant life.

B$LLIONAIRE BAD BOY

Function:

Noun

1. Being disciplined.

2. The most powerful person in the room.

3. The specific mindset and belief designed for creating wealth.

4. Self-awareness and really knowing who you are and what you want to pursue in life.

5. Complete control of time and money and 100% control over what happens in your life.

6. An accumulated attitude and mindset of a level of wealth beyond the ordinary.

"If you have worked for thirty years doing the same shit you've hated day in and day out because you were afraid to quit and take a risk, you've been living like a pussy. Period, point blank. Tell yourself the truth! That you've wasted enough time, and that you have other dreams that will take courage to realize, so you don't have to die a fucking pussy!"

~ David Goggins

Introduction

NO ONE THINKS YOU HAVE THE BALLS TO PULL IT OFF

A great book always begins every success story with the chapter that most advantages itself, so the precipitating chapters are rendered as food for thought, that if used properly, will allow you to pull off the impossible. Having come to a point in my life, far beyond anything that I could have ever imagined, I have spent much of my research searching for and answering the question or questions by which I might fully understand the breach between me and my financial freedom. The time spent studying these questions and a great deal of the time I might add, provided the realization that nobody is coming to make you rich. You aren't fucking drafted. Becoming rich is a choice. It's voluntary. And that makes no sense at all to the rational mind, which is why these four letters (R.I.C.H.) elude so many people. Now, there is nothing surprising about my success because I have always been pedal to the floor. Not over or around, but through. And if I am going to do something, it must be done to death. That's the point of this course, to demonstrate to you the innumerable ways in which you can create the lifestyle that you desire.

You are often told that it only takes one person to make a change, but the only way we can change is to be real with ourselves. So I want you to be 100% yourself because your life story, your knowledge, and your message..what you know from experience and want to share with the world have greater importance and market value than you probably ever dreamed. I share my backstory because I want you to know I have been where you are now. I have struggled to get my message out there, but now I'm here to help you. We are in this together. The only question now is whether you care enough about your self-worth, personal growth, self-reliance and financial freedom to overcome your fears.

You are about to go on an extremely, exciting journey. I know because I did and I loved every second of it. I learned the lessons in this book from experience so I'm here to deliver a different perspective, a model that works. This course is simple. You'll learn how to create a decision-making filter so you can be who you want to be, do what you want to do and have what you want to have. Inside these pages, you won't find self-help jargon and there's no deep theory. Instead, you'll find simple, straight forward ideas and easy-to-implement action steps, written in everyday language by a guy who does it everyday and delivers results. You'll discover a new perspective...a fresh way of filtering all that you do. In the upcoming pages, I'll be asking you to mirror what I did to create your own game within the game, and as you take this course, you'll discover the rewards, freedom, and gratification that give you a sustainable, competitive advantage...a mind-blowing experience. But, this is not about changing your life instantly, it's about moving the needle bit by bit, making those changes sustainable and developing a more productive can-do dialogue with yourself. This is a tactic for you to be your best. More than anything, it will reveal your mindset, which is exactly what it's designed to do. Remember this is a game you are playing within yourself...a war. And this war like most battles we fight in life will be won or lost in your own mind. Becoming a *B$LLIONAIRE BAD BOY* is a mind game and your advantage as a *B$LLIONAIRE BAD BOY* will become clearer with every page of this book.

PART ONE

One flawless chess move after another

Your only real opponent is you, so shape yourself to become your Mentor-In-The-Mirror!

Chapter One

THE RICHEST MOTHERF$CKER THAT YOU WILL EVER MEET IS IN THE MIRROR

(Stop watching other people's lives and start living your own)

Everything is a condition of the mind. The idea comes first and then the manifestation of that idea. You can't be, you can't do and you can't have anything until you first have the idea of it in your mind. Whatever you believe about yourself seals your destiny and whatever you believe about yourself brings you success or failure. This is pure self-psychology. By truthfully answering the following questions you can take your lifestyle and your personal finances to the next level. How you answer these questions will help you identify what's missing in your financial life and help you determine where you want to go, and what resources you need to leverage for help.

- How do you define yourself? (Take some time with this & explain in detail)

- What idea of who you are, are you planting in your mind?

- How important are self-awareness and self-discovery to you?

- How can your definition of yourself help you take control of your life and your finances?

Chapter Two

AUTHORITY NOT BASED ON MERIT, BUT ON SHEER POWER

(Act as a free man while surrounded by walls)

The standard of living you have is all because of the attitude and beliefs you have about yourself. What you believe about yourself determines all the results you have in your life regarding money. Most people have such a deep rooted, small view of themselves that they think money and wealth are out of reach for them. The truth is you can create any amount of wealth you want for yourself, you just have to have the right mindset and attitude for it. By answering the following questions and evaluating your current life experience, it will become clear as to whether or not your efforts are meaningful or whether you must set a new and more proactive course for your life.

- What am I really after in life? (money, freedom, love etc.)

- I believe I can make more money than I do now because?

- What steps can I take today, this week, this month, this year to make this happen?

- When I feel weak and distracted, the reason I will keep going is?

Chapter Three

THE MOST POWERFUL POSITION IN THE WORLD

(Aspire to greatness, even if you do not
achieve fame, success or money)

Often, when we fail to get what we want we look for someone to blame. Sadly, this often leads us to point the finger at others, rather than accept that we are the source of the problem. There are some very important questions that you need to ask yourself, so the following exercise is just one of several you will encounter within this course. These questions will better enable you to determine where you are in life, along with where you would like to be, and what you need to do to get there. Coming up with good answers is far less important than taking the time to ask yourself tough questions, but be sure to answer truthfully. As simple as this may sound, many people are shocked by their answers. These questions are designed to ignite serious introspection, so ask yourself these questions regularly and you will make better, more effective decisions about your life and the actions you need to take.

- What's your definition of freedom? (Take some time with this & explain in detail)

- Can you achieve the freedom(financial or otherwise) that you want by following the masses?

- What do you want your legacy to be...Consumer or Producer?

- Are you willing to challenge traditional assumptions about education, life and work, to discover new solutions that will allow you to shift the balance of power?

- What is your greatest asset?

- How can you use your asset to take control of your life and your circumstances?

PART TWO

The most exclusive level of financial freedom

B$LLIONAIRE BAD BOY

"Damn right I like the life I live, because I went from negative to positive!"

~ Notorious B.I.G.

Chapter Four

WEAR THE CROWN AND ADMIRE
THE WAY IT SPARKLES

(Make a bold power move)

I t's highly possible to take monumental steps toward high levels of prosperity, financial independence and inner peace, with the money you are already bringing home. What could your children and your children's children accomplish if you set your family free from the bondage of debt? By answering the following questions truthfully, you can take your financial life to the next level, and you and your family can be financially secure regardless of a fluctuating economy.

- Can you see how operating on 100 percent cash can benefit you more than using credit? (Save $1000 as fast as you can to use as an emergency fund to cover emergencies with cash without having to go into debt.)

- Are you willing to sell some stuff or work an extra job to do whatever it takes to focus your resources on debt elimination? (Track your spending on items such as food, groceries, insurance, clothes and recreation, to determine where you can cut expenses and determine how much extra money could be applied towards debt elimination.)

- Think about all the money that is currently going out in the form of debt payments (credit cards, furniture, car loans, mortgage, etc.). How would you feel if you actually got to keep all that money every month? What could you do with it? (List all of your debts except your house then prioritize them to pay off the smallest balance through the largest balance.)

- Are you willing to sacrifice extra money to pay the absolute maximum amount that you can until the debt is gone? (Make the regular payment plus the extra money on the smallest balance until it is paid off while making the minimum payments on all of your other debts.)

- Are you willing to discipline yourself to repeat the process again and again until all of your debts have been eliminated? (When the first debt is paid off maintain focus by using the money from the debt you paid off to pay on to the next debt, then the next debt and so on.)

Most people aren't living their life's dreams because they have to pay bills. Imagine having absolutely no debt, no car payments, no credit card payments, or even a house payment. You have the power and the privilege to eliminate your debt and transform your life. Again, if you didn't have to pay bills, what would you do with all that money?

Chapter Five

INVENT MONEY THAT ALREADY EXISTS

(A higher income doesn't
guarantee financial freedom)

The median household income in America is about $59,000. Multiply that by an average 40 year working life and you'll see that the average household will make $2,360,000 in a lifetime. Imagine for a minute what it would be like to keep most of that because you don't have to worry about paying bills. What would that feel like? Who would you be? Ask yourself the following questions to discover the limitless possibilities. These questions will help you focus on what you truly value and what makes your life worth living. The point is to clear out all the distractions and rationalizations and all the bullshit we tell ourselves. Allow yourself to be pissed off and don't give a fuck anymore, but in a positive way. Don't allow your mind to justify your current situation, and over time, amazing changes will occur...not only in your relationship with money, but in your relationship with life itself.

- The amount of my current income is? (Keep in mind that there are people who aren't any smarter than you making billions) How do you feel about making this amount?

- Multiply your annual salary by the number of years you plan to work until you retire. Describe in detail how it would feel to keep most of it because you don't have to pay bills. What would it feel like? Who would you be?

- How does it feel to live like you make less income than you actually do because you're in debt?

- The total amount I pay in bills/owe in debts is? How pissed off are you about having to pay this much? How stupid do you feel about getting into debt?

Write a "I'm pissed off and I don't give a fuck anymore: statement. Example: I'm pissed off and I don't give a fuck anymore...I will not continue to live paycheck to paycheck, losing sleep wondering how I'm going to make ends meet etc. (The more detailed the statement the better)

PART THREE

Capitalistic aspirations

"I like signing million dollar deals. Where's my pen? Bitch I'm signing!"

~ Cardi B

Chapter Six

HEADS I WIN, TAILS I DON'T LOSE

(Always set yourself up to win)

Take a piece of paper and draw a line down the middle. On one side, write down all the subjects you're knowledgeable about. Take some time with this because you know more than you think you do. In the second column, make a similar list of things that you are passionate about. Take a look at your list and see what subject shows up in both columns then do a web search to see who is marketing to your future customers. If your search turns up page after page of commercial sites, congratulations! You just found your niche.

KNOWLEDGE	PASSION

Chapter Seven

THE FEELING OF FLYING WITHOUT
THE FEAR OF FALLING

(Set your sights high and let the world know)

Take an asset and build a system around it. Most people do not know how to set up a business like that. Every problem is a product. Find the problem and sell the solution. This same concept will work for you. The following questions will help you position yourself to develop an Information business and discover your own information product topics and ideas. After you have answered these questions, take it one step further with self-reflection and research, to gain clarity and figure out the best possible direction for you, and then ambitiously pursue your own self-direction. Let the power of your *B$LLIONAIRE BAD BOY* attitude take you where you want to go, do what you want to do and create the lifestyle you want to live.

- The topics I have always studied and been fascinated by are...

- People on social media often dream of achieving…

- Something I have always wanted to learn more about is…

- People on social media are afraid of not knowing enough about…

- Things that I have been through in my life that might inspire people are…

- People on social media often pay good money for…

- The topic I would love to help people with is…

- The thing that seems to frustrate people on social media the most right now is…

- If I could give people I know information that would help them improve their lives, they would probably want strategies on how to...

- Based on my answers to the previous questions, how-to-information that I could provide to people I know that would help them, would include strategies on how to...

Chapter Eight

CREATE YOUR OWN RELIGION

(Be smarter, wiser and do it your way)

The ability to solve problems can make you billions. If you can solve your customer's problems, you could convince them to buy almost anything. By answering the following questions, brainstorming, and some real-life observation, you can develop products by solving problems and selling the solution.

- This product is for: (Who will buy this product? Be specific.)

- It will help them solve this problem: (Describe the problem your customers are looking to solve.)

- I expect my product to: (Explain how your solution will solve their problem in a meaningful and valuable way.)

- This is how I will do this: (What is your strategy?)

PART FOUR

The only voice you need in your head is your own

B$LLIONAIRE BAD BOY!

"I'm bout the stacks...Basically when I say I'm bout the stacks, I mean I'm bout the struggle, I'm about the determination, the hard work, the grind, the hustle, the money. I'm about having dreams and then accomplishing those dreams and making them come to reality."

~ Soulja Boy

Chapter Nine

GAINING & PROTECTING WEALTH
& STATUS...PERMISSION IS NOT REQUIRED

(No matter how someone wants to feel in life,
they want the freedom to feel it)

E very man wants to be the man that he dreams about being, but society makes it easy for us to compromise, and offers us so little that we take anything. You will never be lost if you let the light inside you, guide you. For every dark shadow, there is a shaft of light...a prize for those who want to reach for it. The power of *B$LLIONAIRE BAD BOY* is the dream of what that could be...a symbol of possibility. You don't have to be a genius to make genius moves because each game is different. Simply answer the questions from the previous chapters over and over again and adjust your game accordingly. That's the real definition of being a *B$LLIONAIRE BAD BOY* and owning your destiny. There is so much more that you can achieve if you will only believe that you can. Do you want to be profound? Or do you want to be just another face in the crowd not doing anything? Success comes from saying fuck it, I ain't through just yet, and giving it another go. Even if the difficulty of achievement on a scale of 1-10 appears to be a 10. Dreams are worth more than money and resiliency is what breeds success. As well, reputation is what people think of you, but character is what you are. This is neither philosophy nor a political statement, because we can hunt our dreams with a fierceness unimagined. It's about being so

55

financially literate that they talk about you, invest in you and do business with you...that's the ultimate goal. Allowing you to manage your finances on your own terms, and sell unique, boutique products and services that are customized, hard to find, and nearly impossible to replicate; because you are solving the problems of a customer base that loves you, comes back to you again and again, and tells their friends about you. The culmination of everything that has been bubbling up inside of you under the surface.

LESS BRAVADO MORE WISDOM

I fancy myself a boss...an owner. I'm a serial entrepreneur, and I'm proud of it because I'm a trusted resource for millions of people and a powerful force for good. God has blessed me with a unique ability to defy reality and it feels really good to turn my success and failure into something that helps people around the world, because they don't want handouts...they want to own their own businesses, and to be entrepreneurs. It would be difficult to deny what people worldwide deeply desire. So, what will you do today? What dreams will you chase? What will you do or experience that will help you feel fulfilled and grateful, when you rest your head on your pillow later tonight? Are you prepared to do battle for a dream that is worth dreaming? What ever you do, don't overestimate the competition, and underestimate yourself. Financial freedom doesn't happen by chance. Do not limit your vision based on other's permission. The only permission ever granted by society is permission to follow its norms and traditions. No one will ever grant you permission to advance because they fear being left behind, or made a fool of for clinging to old and traditional methods of chasing the American Dream.

I share this solely for the purpose of showing you that you can create whatever results you want regarding money. With freedom on the line, you would expect that most people would understand that human nature steers us towards self-reliance and economic empowerment. But many remain clueless, reacting to each day of life without power. Thus they are not free...they are slaves.

Getting what you want out of life is not about circumstances. It's about taking responsibility, and overcoming or changing your circumstances. So stop blaming the education system. Stop blaming your employer. Stop blaming the economy. You are responsible for your situation. The day you start blaming yourself in a positive way is the day you are well on your way to becoming a *B$LLIONAIRE BAD BOY.*

CRASH THE PARTY

So here is what I'm going to do for you. I'm going to liven things up. Everything we hear is an opinion, not fact. Everything we see is a perspective, not truth. Our life is what our thoughts make it. Once you come up with an idea, it's just a question of believing in that idea, then riches are possible. *B$LLIONAIRE BAD BOYs* see ourselves as exceptional...the greatest and noblest ever to exist, and we wield this power and control in whatever way is most useful at the moment, to protect our positions. I had seen that dream all my life and wanted to escape into that dream for a long time. But this was never an option, because the dream rested solely on following society's perception of the dream. What we must never do is willingly hand over our freedom. I was freed when I realized that I had the power to truly consider how I wished to live and I answered the question by answering the questions. It was always right in front of me.

PRELUDE TO A DREAM

✓ Being a B$LLIONAIRE BAD BOY begins with ideology!

✓ Being a B$LLIONAIRE BAD BOY is a response to one's own actions, or lack of action!

✓ Being a B$LLIONAIRE BAD BOY is 80 percent behavior and only 20 percent knowledge!

✓ Being a B$LLIONAIRE BAD BOY offers an ambitious person more avenues to economic independence!

✓ Being a B$LLIONAIRE BAD BOY reinforces the message that your experiences and perspectives about wealth are the only ones that matter!

✓ Being a B$LLIONAIRE BAD BOY is open, unending and free. Slowly discovering yourself!

✓ Being a B$LLIONAIRE BAD BOY is the value you hold...how you perceive yourself and are perceived by others, in terms of your power or status!

✓ Being a B$LLIONAIRE BAD BOY is a powerful construct, because it calls out to your deeply internalized sense of superiority and entitlement!

✓ Being a B$LLIONAIRE BAD BOY is a person's internalized awareness of his or her potential!

- ✓ Being a B$LLIONAIRE BAD BOY always manifests itself in action, because the way you see the world drives your actions!

- ✓ Being a B$LLIONAIRE BAD BOY occurs when there is an interruption to that which is familiar and taken for granted!

- ✓ Being a B$LLIONAIRE BAD BOY is a legitimization of one's entitlement to resources, it can also be defined as permission to escape or avoid any challenges to this entitlement!

At any moment in life, you can become a *B$LLIONAIRE BAD BOY* because it's a belief system and a way of looking at the world. This course was designed to make visible the relentless messages of being a *B$LLIONAIRE BAD BOY,* and the resulting, inevitable internalization of these messages. Most people never find themselves with this protection. If they do, it is because they have chosen to step outside their area of safety. It is not the mere presence of the *B$LLIONAIRE BAD BOY* mindset, but the ambition, drive, purpose, and aspirations it demands. Because it requires repetition that produces thoughts, perceptions, expressions and actions that become your familiar way of perceiving, interpreting and responding to the social cues around you. I strategically guide people to a shared understanding of what I mean by these claims. My own experience and strategy put people's overall reception of me light years beyond how I was received in the early days. I am offering you a teachable moment and I am only asking that you listen with openness, because my only goal in creating this course was to match your ambition, aggression, and intelligence with your *B$LLIONAIRE BAD BOY* mindset. The entire course doesn't have to make sense to you. It just needs to position you to expand your concept of money...end of discussion.

THE LIFE OF WHICH AT ONE
TIME YOU COULD ONLY DREAM

I can't make you wealthy by giving you a handout, but I can place you on the road to prosperity by teaching you what I know. Inside each of us is a *B$LLIONAIRE BAD BOY*, but to become a *B$LLIONAIRE BAD BOY*, you need to decide what is best for you. You need to decide what you want to learn, and what you'll need to unlearn. You must pursue what you truly want out of life and not what others want you to pursue because we are all different. We have different gifts, intelligence, and different dreams and you can rest assured that you will never attain true happiness if you wait for others to show you the way. Whether you are black or white, male or female, married or single, tall or short, rich or poor, have a high school diploma or are highly educated, you are in charge of whether you get there. The game of money is just that...a game. You will go crazy if you don't realize that, and you can not win unless you have a clear sense of what success means to you.

The deepest personal defeat suffered by human beings, is constituted by the difference between what one is capable of becoming and what one has in fact become. In my work to constantly increase my own financial literacy, I have found that answering these questions never failed me, and I have no plans to change the way I operate. I decided what was best for me, and I decided that economic empowerment would take me where I wanted to go. This choice inspired me to be the best I could be, and now it's time for you to decide what's best for you. Life is about choices, and when you position yourself as a *B$LLIONAIRE BAD BOY*, you give yourself the advantage of being able to see that traditional thinking is a completely opposite path to a life of self-reliance and economic empowerment. Dreams often come true for many people, but only for those who focus and work on them.

This is your moment of power, the answer and the key to your freedom. By educating yourself about how money works, you unlock the potential within yourself to break free from the mentality of mediocrity, and see abundance all around you. The terms and rules may be a little different, but the basic concepts are true all over the world. This understanding is freeing because it allows you to focus on how, rather than if, and this message circulates 24-7 with intention, awareness, and agreement.

Throughout this book, I have attempted to make visible the inevitable patterns displayed by self-reliant people. When these patterns are named or questioned, we have predictable responses. The responses begin with a set of examined assumptions, which when questioned, trigger various emotions and activate expected behaviors. These behaviors are then justified by numerous claims, and these responses, emotions, behaviors and claims are illustrated. So, the final advice I offer is this: Take the initiative and find out on your own. You are growing into a consciousness, and my wish for you is that you feel no need to constrict yourself. I'm convincing millions of people to change their lives...to become *B$LLIONAIRE BAD BOY*s. Are you next?

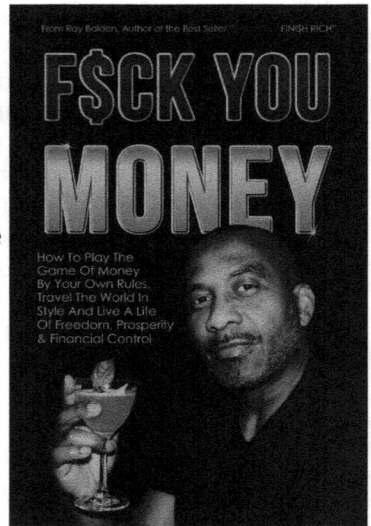

From RAY BOLDEN, Author of the Best Seller "BAD BOYS FINI$H RICH"

A BOOK FOR A VIDEO

BE A PART OF THE THOUSANDS OF LIVES CHANGED WITH THE HELP OF THE BAD BOYS FINI$H RICH PRINCIPLES!

Here's How It Works:

1. Once you receive your book, create a video of you holding up the book and enthusiastically saying the following:

I'm (First & Last Name) from (City & State or City and Country)!
"Bad Boys or Bad Girls" Finish Rich! (Based on your gender)
I Got My Copy, Get Yours!

2. Post the video on social media (youtube.com, instagram, facebook etc.)

3. Email the link of your video to admin@badboysfinishrich.com.

Once we receive your video link and verify it for clarity and authenticity, we will add it to our growing list of videos.

Please Note: Please follow the script provided above. We reserve the right to reject and refuse any videos deemed substandard or inappropriate.

Visit **BADBOYSFINISHRICH.COM**
for examples!

FOLLOW RAY ON SOCIAL MEDIA

PERSPECTIVES ON FINANCIAL LITERACY AND ENTREPRENEURIAL EDUCATION THAT OFTEN CONTRADICT CONVENTIONAL WISDOM

Follow Ray on Facebook:

www.facebook.com/boldambitionworldwide

Follow Ray on Instagram:

www.instagram.com/badboysfinishrich

Follow Ray on Amazon:

www.amazon.com/Ray-Bolden/e/B00VXC3YN4/ref=ntt_dp_epwbk_0

Please Note: After enjoying Ray's work, please provide a customer review and give feedback on Amazon.com.

Visit **BADBOYSFINISHRICH.COM**

BAD BOYS FINI$H RICH

BOLD AMBITION
WORLDWIDE